Village Talk

A collection of poems

By Arielle Deseré

VILLAGE TALK

Copyright © 2024 Arielle Deseré

For More Information,

Email: arielledc@gmail.com

Instagram: @arielledesere

Website: www.arielledesere.com

Scripture quotations marked (ESV) are from The ESV® Bible (The Holy Bible, English Standard Version®), © 2001 by Crossway, a publishing ministry of Good News Publishers. Used by permission. All rights reserved.

Scripture quotations taken from The Holy Bible, New International Version® NIV® Copyright © 1973, 1978, 1984, 2011 by Biblica, Inc. Used with permission. All rights reserved worldwide.

DEDICATION

Glory to God! The day you touched me forever changed my life. I refuse to go back to the sandy shore. Even if I have to kick like hell to swim in the deep, I'll choose to be wherever you are.

To the first member of The Village, Avi, thank you for always believing.

To my husband, thank you for loving me from broken, to whole. I love you deeply.

To my Mama, in 22 short years you prepared me for an entire lifetime. I couldn't have possibly been blessed with a better mother.

To Nana, you knew I could do it. Thank you for speaking new possibilities.

Dad (I'm your Forever Child), Grandparents, Auntie Connie, Auntie Marilyn, many CLOSE Aunts and Uncles. Thank you for investing your love into me. We did it!

Gabriella, Mommy always wants to make you as proud of me as I am of you. I adore you. You have awakened inside of me the fiercest writer that I've ever been. When I'm long gone, you'll have the deepest parts of my heart in here. I trust The Village to remind you of the words I shared.

Emiliano, my nephew and "first born." You inspired me to dream big for the future of little brown children. Tita is getting the world ready for you.

And to The Village: Nelly, BFFH, LBG, 6H, Dearest Friends, Ferm, Godbrother, Godsister, Godmother, Family-In-Love, Cousins, Mentors, Mentees, Sisters & Brothers in Christ, Aunts and Uncles, Miss Allyson, Extended Family, Norfolk State Spartans, DVHS, San Diego Aztecs, and everyone that has opened their eyes and ears to my work. I love you. This is for The Village!

Table of Contents

The Skin I'm In (2024)

I decided to accept the woman that I am
And the warm brown beautiful skin that I'm in
No.
I've decided to *love* the woman that I am
And the insecure woman within.
I don't always wake up with a smile right away
Sometimes, when I'm looking deep in my face
I look in the mirror
and beyond the pretty, is still plenty
Plenty flaws and
plenty hate
Plenty man I wish
Decisions that I made
Chances I had to take
Physical choices I made
that I wish I hadn't made
Thoughts behind the emotions
that are never given voices
All of it shaping me into the woman I am today
Take a look at this brown skin
It clings to me
Whether I gain weight
or lose it and get lean
It's there

Arielle Deseré

And there is no denying or passing
So, I uplift it
Proud of the legacy I'm representing
I'm Black
It's who I am, it's what I love
Just as much as I am woman
Just as much as I am Christian
My color is my culture
Something I don't plan on forgetting
Every part of me
Every stereotype
I don't regret it
'Cause like my hair,
My head is Big
My confidence intimidates the weak
The audacity of me to see the system
and find ways to not fall at its feet
I may not be light enough for you
I wasn't born for your impressions
I don't seek affirmations from anywhere but the Word
I'm not European
and I don't subscribe to European beauty lessons
I look East African, but thanks to slavery
your guess is as good as my guess is.
What I know?

Village Talk

The rings around my eyes say I come from a line of the
restless
Something ancient and passed down
So, I count it as something I'm blessed with
Stories in these eyes say I've been here before
I've seen some things I wish I hadn't
It's imprinted on my irises
But the knowledge replicates and my mission
is to spread it like viruses
I am, a woman of the nations
Blacker than your assessment
Made by the omnipresent
Designed in his very presence
Called and anointed
Dare I say even destined
I'm not there yet.
I'm not even close to being perfected,
but I'm refined.
Out of the ashes and the coal,
a diamond is being mined
But though I haven't yet arrived
I am decided
I am sure
That the woman I am today
deserves to be adored.

Arielle Deseré

Have You Ever Been a Black Woman?

Have you ever been a Black woman?
Let's talk about it.
There are many hats that women wear,
but we wear the whole damn suit.
Is this a safe space?
Baby I'm tired of working.
I have one,
two,
damn three many jobs.
I just wanna come home and cut the game on too.
What if I didn't have to multitask during my commute?
Riding on the train home thinking
about what we were going to eat.
Or if my Sundays,
weren't spent in the grocery store
and over the washing machine.
I would have a whole lot more time
to kickback and be me.
Have you ever been a Black woman?

So YES you gon' pay for these nails.
You gon' pay for these feet.
You gon' drop $200 once a month
to wine and dine me.

Village Talk

Just to pay for all the things I do for you
that you don't see.
Like keeping a full fridge
and toilet paper on the roll.
Making sure the light bill is paid.
And our water stays on.
Putting the leftovers up.
Cleaning the microwave.
Asking you "How was work?"
even though I had a bad day.
Have you ever been a Black woman?

It's a silent scream!
Look how I held us down.
Look how we all matching and smiling
for the picture of our family.
You think that came easy?
Baby I'm working when I get home.
I'm working when I wake up.
I'm working when I'm in the bathroom alone.
I'm working for us because
the world don't want us to be.
Have you ever been a Black woman?

Being your safe space.
Even though I know I don't have a space

to call my place.
Oooh to be a Black woman.
I'm fighting for you and me.
I'm fighting everybody that's against the Black family.
I'm uplifting our children, you, myself.
Who's uplifting me?
I'm uplifting me.
I got us.
You got me,
but I got us.
Thank you for all you do,
but hold on
let me talk about what I need.
Have you ever been a Black woman?

I hope now you see me.
Everybody talks about how hard the Black man has it,
but we don't get a break.
We don't get us time.
We don't get a man cave.

So, what do I need?
I need what I ask
when I ask it
because dare I even ask it.
I deserve to be paid.

Village Talk

I deserve to be called
by my God given name.
I need more than the white woman
because all the pressure is on me.
I'm the anchor, I'm the rock, I'm the sta-bil-ity.
But I'm supposed to stay silent?
NO
I need what I need
when I ask for what I need
WHEN I ask it
because...
Have you ever been a Black woman?

Huh!
I hope now, you feel me.

Daddy Issues

I was just waiting for him to come
Standing
Watching
It taught me to accept commitment issues
I was just practicing patience
Calling
Longing
Waiting
Developing low expectations.

Fathers Wanted

Daddy wassup?
Seems like when I call
sometimes you don't pick up
And I know being a father is a lot to ask for,
but being brought into this world
aint what I asked for

Daddy, I need your time and attention
because when you don't want to
some young man is trying to give it
Are you listening to me?
'Cause I need you to realize
Look Daddy I am of your flesh
Look Daddy I have your eyes

I don't call you for money
I don't want none
I'd rather have a broke daddy
than a part time one

I'm so smart and independent
and you don't even see
That I cry all the time because you don't have time
and I'm not as strong as I try to be

9

and Mama can't be Mama
and be Daddy

I do have the LORD as my father
and he's the best dad
I could ever have
But he placed you
to be here for me
on his behalf
So that I could have someone
to look up to
So that when I get married
my husband would be just like you

Isaiah 32:8 says, "He who is noble
does noble things and on noble things
he stands."
So, when I say fathers wanted
I'm saying, Daddy
I need you to be a noble man.

Forever Child

There is still so much I don't know
Like a youngster,
I'm excited when you teach me
So much to be gained from the love of a father
Affirmation from being secured
Joy from making you proud
Supported
Outwardly
Visually
Loved wide enough to submerge past pains
Presence
I soak it in and bloom from the light
It's warm here
Stay with me
Let's grow together
Father and daughter
There's much to be gained here
You have secrets of life
Wisdom
I have secrets of youth
Passion
I am humbled
Grateful
Christ laid this glue

Arielle Deseré

Christ drew us close to whisper secrets
To teach intimacy
As we heal,
let it harden from resin to rock
Let it mature and reach the heavens
Like redwoods reaching up
Swaying, dancing
Praising the Lord together
For His mercy lasts a lifetime
And in His presence is wholeness
Stay with me
And live long
There's honor that is due
Earthly Abba,
I want to honor you.

Black Man,

Black man I fight for you
Past your traumas
I'll never give up
My hands won't go up in surrender
Succumbing to the intentional attacks
planned on our families
the brokenness
No, I won't fold
I will stand front line
Shotgun or picket sign
I will keep fighting
Won't you fight for me?

Arielle Deseré

Safe Me Brother – A letter to my brother

I don't feel safe
when I'm with you brother.
I treat you like my brother,
but you act like we don't descend from the same mother.
I can't relax around you
when I should feel peace.
I feel tense when I walk past you.
You attack me if I do or don't speak.
I speak out the loudest for you.
You're quiet when they wrong me.
I feed you and offer my bosom
to you brother.
You show me your back
and your feet.
You mock when I pass you.
You won't uplift me.
Won't call me a genius
unless it's your sport that I beat.
As if my art, my work, my lane is minuscule
and you could be me.
I see you,
three lone brothers in the back
that greet me as Queen.
It's your brothers next to you Brother.

Village Talk

The ones that don't care for their seeds.
The ones you play ball with
and pretend not to see.
When they berate and harass, demean
and rape me.
When they judge my dress, label,
and lie on me.
Your brother, my brother,
our brothers I mean.
Speak out for me brother.
Advocate for your queen.
Choose up for me brother.
Your protection I need.
Your love I need
Your allyship I need
Your energy I need
Your comfort I need
Your warmth I need
Your voice I need
Your kinship I need
You Brother, to level up and succeed.
I need you brother.
Hold me down.
Safe me.

Arielle Deseré

Before We Talk Peace

Dedicated to the mothers of Oscar Grant, Miles Hall, George Floyd (Late), Breonna Taylor, and every mother that had to fight against the justice system for the justice of their child.

Respectfully, I don't want any more condolences.
Sorry is not enough to atone for my loss.
What I want is not an ask.
It's a demand, it's a triumph, it's a radicalization, it's a decree
it's a victory.
I'm here for JUSTICE.
And I won't stop until justice is what I see.

No! I don't want a building or a street or a mural
or a scholarship.
I'm here for JUSTICE.
And I won't stop until justice is what I see.

That means killers in cages, suspensions without wages,
history of past violences kept in public databases.
I'm here for JUSTICE.
And I won't stop until justice is what I see.

What do I imagine when I think of public safety
sounds a lot to me like I have a dream.

Village Talk

But we're sixty years past dreaming
and 200 years and some change
past let freedom ring.
Stop silencing me with reform
and give me humanity!
I'm losing brothers to troubled brothers,
I'm losing brothers to crowded prisons,
I'm losing brothers to the hands of public safety!
How many more brothers?
How many more sisters?
How many more mothers have to lose their babies?
I'm here for JUSTICE.
And I won't stop until justice is what I see.

Give me funded rec centers,
give me sports for our children,
I want band rooms,
I want trade schools,
I want opportunity.
I want Black history taught in class,
I want trips to the museum,
I want tennis,
I want swim class.
I want our children to dream.
I'm here for JUSTICE.
And I won't stop until justice is what I see.

That means police out of schools,
that means knees off our necks,
that means public safety officers actually knowing
and having respect in our communities.
That means accountability.
That means persecution.
That means Justice!
That means Justice!
That means JUSTICE
before peace.

March

I don't have to know you
You look like me
You fell at the same hands I suffer from
Oppression
Hands I may fall at
Even on your behalf
But for you, I will fall
I will stick out my wrist
I will ball up my fists
Put your name on my lips and lift
Until hoarse
Until in the ground stiff
March for you and me
And all of our children
With them on my hip
And my shoulders
I will rally
Always.

Arielle Deseré

They Want Us in Chains

They want us in chains
I said they want us in chains.
They want us in chains
Crated and locked away
Behind bars, behind gates, labeled enemy of the state
We are prisoners, we are workers, we are criminals,
we are slaves
As soon as the shackles came off,
they calculated how much they could make
if they put us away
Designed a system that would seal our fate
and snatch food from our families' mouths
and onto their plates
They want us in chains
I said they want us in chains.

From childhood they marched us into classes single file
and punished us every time
we laughed and cracked smiles
Each head in that class
has a dollar tag attached to their feet
So, your child had better have their ass in that seat
Sit still, look straight,
and don't you dare speak

Village Talk

'Cause when your brown baby acts wild,
their teacher is calling the campus police
When he comes, he's going to ask you to spit
that school number ID
That community officer is not there
to help keep the peace
But to introduce your child to the system
for when he's caught on the street
Don't believe me?
Ask how many white kids have met school officers
versus kids that are Black like me
They want us in chains
I said they want us in chains.

The first time they catch you in the streets
you don't catch a break
Your stint in Juvie
is setting you up for the county
and a system full of hate
Now every time you leave your house
is a risk that you'll take
A simple traffic stop now quickly escalates
Have a seat on the curb
as they dare you to give them a reason to retaliate
Now a broken taillight
has earned you a ticket to a trip upstate

Next thing you know you look up
and you've been doing 10 years behind gates
They want us in chains
I said they want us in chains.

They gave drugs to our communities
and then blamed it on us
Calling it self-hatred as if it wasn't taught
As if the system hasn't created ways
for us to be caught
Once you get out, try finding a job
Your rights are taken so you can't affect laws
'Cause they don't want you to vote
for your sheriff and DA
And they don't want you to vote
to take school police away
'Cause to them
we are prisoners
we are workers
we are criminals
we are slaves
They want us in chains
I said they want us in chains.

They want us in chains
I said they want us in chains.
But we will be freed.

Arielle Deseré

Little Black Girl

For Gabby

Little Black girl in a little black world
don't let it dim your light.
Little Black girl in a little black world,
remember that you are the light.
This little black world watches its little Black girl
to see what she'll do.
It takes what you create.
It mocks and provokes you.
Then turns it around
and blames your reactions on you.

Take your torch little Black girl
and hold it up high.
Hold it high as your head.
Use your flame to burn it all down to the ground.
If it rebuilds burn it down again.
This little black world must never forget
who truly wears the crown.
It must not forget your resilience.
This little black world was never yours,
Little Black girl
but you are what makes it spin.

24

Village Talk

Tell the little black world
it can try and try
but it will not and cannot exist
If it will not share the power,
cages you in,
and refuses to let you win.

Little Black Girl in a little black world,
don't let it dim your light.
Little Black girl in a little black world,
remember that you are the light.
Use your torch little Black girl.
Hold it up high.
Hold it as high as your head.
Don't hold back little Black girl.
Now it's your turn. Now it's your turn to win.

Draw back little Black girl. Show it why.
Show it why it can spin.
Swing hard little Black girl,
swing hard little Black girl.
Swing hard and do it again.

Swing hard little Black girl with all your might.
Show this little black world how good you can fight.
This little black world will not and cannot exist.

Arielle Deseré

If it holds you back, cages you in,
and refuses to let you win.

Little Black girl in a little black world
don't let it dim your light.
Little Black girl in a little black world,
remember: You are the light.

DNA Story

My skin so tough,
The sky's hottest beams can't burn me.
I got scars from head to toe that tattletale my origin story.
I got broken bones from sticks and stones,
but it's abandonment that really hurt me.
Pain not shown through tears in public,
but translated in my DNA story.

It looks like high blood pressure.
It's eaten until diabetes.
It's blacking out while binge drinking
and shooting loved ones of my enemies.
Re-lived scenes of my grandmother's dreams time-traveling
to 2023
just to haunt me.
The other day,
I had a dream
that 5 Black overseers beat up a man named Tyre Nichols.
He was no bigger than me.
And those 5 Black men hid behind big bad badges
that say they the police.
They hated themselves so much
that they couldn't stop themselves from self-harming.

But that was just a nightmare.
We no longer live there.

Things aint as bad as it seems.
And though I can't unsee it
and lose myself from time to time,
my trauma aint PTSD.
I'm no different than a soldier losing his brother on the
battlefield.
Except, I'm losing mine on the streets.
But move along kids.
Cuff your hands to your eyes.
There's nothing here to see.
Just smoke and mirrors hiding the circus of our un-real reality.
Heaven knows.
We are the sun-kissed stepchildren of America.
But make no mistake, our fairytale ends like Cinderella.
Because even in our dusty cellar, we find a way to make it
better.
Our minds as bright and creative as a throwback Coogi
sweater.
Our defense as resounding as earth's global warning weather.
Because after remembering that no one is coming to save us,
we turn into go-getters.
History tried to hide it, but we always fight back.
We blossom by lifting each other up.
We've always done that.
Black power means no health care,
we'll come to each other.

Village Talk

One has the gift of listening.
The other has the gift to speak comfort.
Another's hugs bring healing
like the prayers of a church mother.
Connected, we have the tools we need
to heal one another.

Our kids can bring their education back to the block
where they come from.
As a unit, we can provide opportunities.
When we don't have, we make one.
How do we heal?
Like we always do.
Get it out before it gets you.
Scream it out through your passions
so the darkness doesn't just feed on you.
Fight against the pain by using it to inspire you.

There is freedom in the arts.
Your voice can move systems when you write out loud.
Watch your power unfold when you give your gifts to a
crowd.
Create the space that is needed for lost youth to be found.
The world is waiting for you to design that new look
and new sound.

Do you know how many generational curses will be broken
when you spread your financial knowledge around?
Who said you can't build a lab in the hood

and train your people up from the ground?
We were chained when we were brought here,
and through that we'll forever be bound.
It started as a curse, but we made it a blessing.
How?
Because we descend from the same people that took scraps
that were thrown on the ground
And turned them into soul food.
Look who wants us a piece now.
We cannot be destroyed.
Only fractured, only broken.
Because what lives in us is creation.
We're self-healing. Self-evolving.

My skin so tough,
the sky's hottest beams can't burn me.
Growing roses through concrete.
It's in our DNA story.

Fight Back

It's not enough to scream
And yell and protest
It's not enough to start a riot
A boycott, a rebellion.
At some point, you have to build your own.
Broaden your shoulders
Stand on ten toes
Assemble your army
And prepare
To protect the throne.

Arielle Deseré

Urban Legend –
Ways and Means to Survive

Legend has is it,
one day we'll all be free.
Well, I don't know about y'all, but I know about me.
I'm not waiting for freedom 'cause freedom aint free.
And I don't know about y'all, but I'm getting mine.
Make it an urban legend.
Ways and means to survive.

The people in my house, I'ma make sure that we're fine.
Once we're good, I'm calling my sister to make sure that they
ate.
Then I'm calling my auntie and bringing over some plates.
Next, I'm calling my homies with the same message to relay.
Put your home back together.
We got moves to make.
And we can't do it if we're all looking our own way,
But before I start stretching and preaching,
I'ma make sure that my house is straight.

See I don't know about y'all, but I'm getting mine.
I'm not waiting for the revolution to be streamed or
televised.

Village Talk

I'm starting my own business and leaving this slave drive.
Now you can keep picking this cotton or you can fall right in
line.
Bring all your gifts with you.
Your ideas and designs.
We're digging up our ancestors' dreams
and bringing them back alive.
I refuse to keep fighting an uphill battle against a system that
never
had me in mind.

We were never in America's wildest dreams supposed to be
free.
Now let that sink in,
Temporarily free.
Let them old families tell it, the south was supposed to win.
And they have a little saying that goes, "the south will rise again."
They can huff and can puff but not by the hairs
on my chinny chin chin.

Me and my house will do more than survive.
It's going to take everybody's brains and everybody's might.
But liberation sounds gooood
when you've been oppressed all your life.

We're planning for retirement and for generations down the line.

Say it with me "Life Insurance" 'cause we all have to die.
We will do more than succeed.
We will thrive and provide.

We're paying off debt and sitting on down.
I'm clearing my schedule to make sure I'm around.
To educate my daughter on her history and all about being
brown.
Because these public schools are stretched too thin
and ran into the ground
for me to trust that in 8 hours
she's not being brainwashed and beaten down.
Imagine spending twice as long to convince her
that her hair is her crown.
And that in Africa, science math and the arts
is where origins have been found.

But if we start at the home, we can create our own rules.
'Cause I don't want those glass ceilings
trying to crack my prized jewel.
Think ahead.
Imagine if we created a network to fund our own schools.

At home, I'm teaching her independence
but to trust, depend, and uplift her Black man.

Village Talk

And what it means to budget every cent that falls into her
hand.
Her home unit is her base and she can't build if her
foundation
is not solid where it stands.

See I don't know about yall, "but I'm leaving here with
somethin'."
We talk 401Ks, stocks, ETFs around here.
And borrowing against life insurance in retirement years.
Making a dollar stretch with 20 dollars to your name.
Having multiple streams of income to support power plays.
The first piece of land takes sacrifice.
The second piece paves the way.
To a future of opportunity attached to your family name.

In the land of the free and the home of the brave,
it's money and land that keeps extinction at bay.
As long as you have land, you get a say.
And together, we'll handle any attacks coming our way.
We can't let fear keep us from moving forward
to achieve something great.
We gotta get our houses in order.
We got moves to make.
'Cause legend has is it,
one day we'll all be free.

Arielle Deseré

I'm not waiting for freedom 'cause freedom aint free.

I'm taking freedom by force for my whole family.
Together, we'll create the opportunity.
Our ancestors got it rolling. It's on us to keep going.
See I don't know about y'all, but I'm getting mine.
Make it an urban legend. Ways and means to survive.

Village Talk

I want to heal together
Not in the dark
What I pour out,
Illumination of my healing
It's invested wealth from the kingdom,
bubbling over
Every encouraging word is seed
Planted
An elder came by with water
A little one pounded the soil
The LORD said, now "Be fruitful"
Reproduce.
Receive it, Village
Pass it around
It's for all of us.

For Us

I grew up being told not to tell all our family business.
And when mama said what she said,
when she said it, she meant it.
So, forgive me if it takes a while for me to tell you
who all I live with.
And all of the things that happened to me
in the house that I lived in.
It's not that I don't believe in mainstream therapy.
I just feel more comfortable relating amongst the people that have
been there with me.
Because to talk healing, you must understand what I deal with.
Being profiled, discriminated,
kids losing friends in the trenches.
Parents that don't live to see old age
due to stress, addiction, and sickness.
My mama died at 47.
I'm here to stand as her witness.
I come from a beautiful Black people,
both vulnerable and strong.
We have been used and manipulated breaking our trust for so long.
But we are the epitome of resilient.

Village Talk

Because despite years of trauma and neglect,
we remain the innovators to contend with.
To influence, change, encourage, and nurture.
Out here fighting our own demons
while still pushing forward the culture.
We've learned to cope by linking arms with our brothers.
We may not have access to mental health resources,
But we have each other.
We push church every Sunday to repent the error of our
ways.
And when one of us falls sick,
we all kneel down and pray.
We sip wine with our sisters as we wind down from our day.
Or gather in hair parlors to laugh and relate.
These are our safe spaces
where we're safe to dream.
So, building our trust means strengthening our community.
Creating programs to not only listen,
but prepare and Uplift.
That address our immediate needs.
Then push for progress.
Here,
within our own community walls
Not always on a couch
or on a hotline call.
Yes, we need to talk through our healing

But an emergency session's not enough.
Because when I go back home
My life is still tough.
To fully heal, we need our neighbors to do the work.
And we can do that by using our gift of innovation
to make mental health centers serving healing FOR US.
Imagine if we had funding for the things that we need.
Support groups for those who've lost loved ones to the streets.
A smash room to get out frustrations, fears, and anxieties.
More boxing gyms than liquor stores on the corners of our
streets.
Mentors walking, not just preaching put the guns down and fight.
Places to release our emotions over an open mic.
Meditation rooms for prayer and to find inner peace.
And centers treating gun violence victims for PTSD.
They say we should seek therapy.
That's the first step, I agree.
But we have to all come to the table if we desire to be free.
'Cause we can heal on our own,
but what's the use when you keep getting beaten down
by a broken community.
Without all of us, our communities will continue to grieve.
As cultural innovators, this is our opportunity
to build safe places to heal that WE can trust.
So, as we look to the world's picture of mental health,
let's rewrite healing and therapy for us.

"You Need to Heal"

Your mama never healed.
Your daddy never healed.
They passed down what they inherited.
Settle in and suppress
with the rest of us.
Why ever, would you tell your business to a stranger?
To an outsider
without rose-colored lenses.

Black Therapy

They say I should seek therapy.

I don't need that.

How do I tell my therapist I'm suffering from being Black?

I'm suffering, 'cause I'm Black.

I'm suffering, and I'm Black.

I'm suffering, but I'm Black.

I'm suffering.

Doctor, it's gon' take more than a session

to meet me where I'm at.

I feel frustrated and

I can't watch the news

Because I'm triggered.

Walking down the street don't know if I'm the next victim.

I need help.

But will you listen?

I need help.

Do you hear me?

People around me keep dying and I'm supposed to go on

living.

Is this how life should be?

At home they're talking at me sharing wisdom.

I hear them, but do they hear me?

I tell them I'm doing good because I know they won't feel me.

They tell me, I'm gon' be alright.

But "I'm gon' be alright" got me crying like every night.
Can you listen?
I need an ear.
Can you listen?
I need to feel.
I go to work and work twice as hard
to get half of my colleagues.
Then I drive home to be pulled over
because they can't believe I can afford what I'm driving.
And I got my mama on speaker 'cause I'm not sure
if I'll be surviving.
Is this the life that you're living?
'Cause I'm tired of being strong.
Them telling me not to cry makes me feel
like my emotions are wrong.
I've been holding the weight of the world for
WAY TOO LONG.
When is it okay to say, I don't feel safe?
Without hearing, boy BACK IN MY DAY...
Well, maybe that's why Daddy left.
Maybe that's why my cousin is on drugs.
Maybe that's why Papa can't climb out the hole that he's dug
and instead, he's drinking himself to death
'cause he don't know how to speak up.
I need help.
Do you hear me?

I need help.
Won't you feel me?
I'm scared they gon' tell me I'm crazy.
So, I'm keeping the thoughts inside.
The medicine makes me feel funny.
So, I'm self-medicating to shield my pride.
I'm eating so I don't cry.
I'm smoking to stay alive.
I'm smiling through my pain while masking thoughts of
suicide.
All this because I can't speak.
But I know I'm doing right
'cause when I cry out, they tell me
nothing's wrong with me.
I need help.
Do you hear me?
I need help.
Won't you feel me?
I been praying, I been fasting
and He told me it's okay to seek therapy.
So, I'm here fighting these stigmas so someone will hear me.
They say I should seek therapy.
Okay, maybe I need that.
But how do I tell my therapist
I'm suffering from being Black?

Open Ears

I never want to receive word saying,
You're gone
No, not another one.
I want to hear you
Even in your actions
Even if you can't speak.

Arielle Deseré

Letter to My Loved Ones

I've heard whispers that Black people don't commit suicide.
I really wish that were true.

Hey Loved One,
So that I don't have to write to you a letter later
I'm telling you now.
You keep asking me and I don't think I can
keep
pushing you out.
You wanna know how I'm doing?
Are you really listening?
If I tell you all my feelings
and I tell them to you clearly...
Do you promise not to tell me to be strong?
Alright, here it goes,
I'll try not to be long.
"I'm...fine. How are you?"
You ask me again as if you can see that I'm blue
So, I repeat it again
because I don't know how to break through
The lifetime indoctrination of pretending to be
cool.

'Cause I don't want to burden others
with the burden of my truth.

Village Talk

But if you could hear my thoughts, I feel alone.
Nobody understands my way of my thinking.
I'm different, and since no one can relate
I prefer sleeping.
I'm moody, throwing tantrums,
crying out like a toddler
that can't communicate what they're feeling.
How am I doing?
I drown out my sorrows with the music of my faves.
They pop pills, do a line and laugh their troubles away.
And I wonder if I follow suit, will I feel the same.
I'll fake it for now
Like everybody else who's smiling
and getting likes on their page.
No, I don't know how to log out
but I know how to isolate.
Alone like these demons want me to be
Locked away in my room.
I say I just want to sleep.
'Cause truth is, I'm worn down of feeling like
in this world it's only me.
How am I doing?
Right now, I need a friend.
Someone to relate to my pain.
Tell me that sometimes, oftentimes
you too have bad days.

And that it's okay to talk to somebody
if I'm feeling the same.
Right now, I need a friend.
Somebody to help.
Tell me that you love that I'm different
And teach me how to love myself.
It's not your fault that I'm feeling this way.
And it's not your fault
that I don't know how to say
all the things that I'm thinking
in my mind everyday.
I want to get better and I'm practicing
by writing it down on the page.
So that I don't have to write to you a letter later,
I'm telling you now.
You keep asking me and I don't think I can keep
pushing you out.
You wanna know how I'm doing?
Well, today is the day.
Today is the day I'm gonna tell you,
"I am not doing okay"
Will you hear me?

Which Direction is Success?

I didn't think I'd be here
The hardest thing about adulthood is sober reality
The lies told in youth about the future,
either manifest or fizzle
There is no riddle
Only is, or unreal
Stand in it
Satisfied or pivot
Envelop in the unrest
I didn't think I'd be here
Which direction is success?

Worthy

Content with less than
Accepting that where I was, was his will
All a plot to keep me from growing and trying to build
Crushing every dream before it anchored
Cursing down passions
"fixing them"
deforming them
Until they were cankered
Seeing them as impossible to thrive
Altering my choices in the name of "staying alive"
Suppression had me thinking I was healed
Suppression had me telling lies
"I'm okay."
I don't need to cry
You call me Princess
I don't see one here
A royal priesthood?
I argue with you as if your word is unclear
Help me look in the mirror
and see perfection
Like you see her
Because I only see less than
Fix my eyes
Fix my esteem

Village Talk

To see the lioness that you named me to be
I wanna look at me and see
Worthy.

None Greater

Debt.
It's disabling.
It's shaming.
It's nagging
like a monkey on my back
that just won't stop complaining.
I feel stuck.
Like every blessing I receive is nice
But being content, I just can't muster up.
'Cause it simply on surface, just isn't enough.
Counting on promotion
Still counting,
No luck.
Mountains and mountains of negatives
got me contemplating using my daughter's stuff.
Like, forget her future.
I can always build her savings back up.
What about all the dreams I have for her to not start off in
this rut?
Do I steal from God?
Just for a little while.
Do I sell all my stock just to feel like
I'm closing in on these rocks that have piled
up with depression?

Village Talk

This guilty feeling like I need to vent in confession.
Battling generational curses.
Still waiting 'til it's time for my blessing.
Still waiting.
All I ever known was broke.
Now here I am, in that exact same boat.
Mama used to say it was hard,
carrying her debt around like a tote.
I vowed to never live that life.
Stashing money in different places just in case things got tight.
Find myself, going into those places often
'cause my balance aint right.
The debt just gnaws at me, attacking my mind.
All of it making me regret my whole life.
When I don't, just wishing I studied law
instead of a dream that's gone up into smoke.
Now I'm catching rain drops from cracks in the ceiling
that can't get patched up with hope.
Praying for relief from my father and
he keeps telling me he'll make it enough.
And I'm making it.
Got barely enough.
But I know barely is better than some.
Except my credit cards tell the story
that my cash flow will never be up.
I ask God for increase

He tells me to use the gifts that he gave me.
I need money and he says,
write poetry and make it amazing.
But what about these bills?
He says you have the gift of expressing what's real.
Most people hold in their trauma when you write it you feel.
Teach my people this expression,
speak the truth and they'll heal.
Words have power
and speaking life for your soul is that nourishing meal.
See my people, touch my people, and let go of your dreams.
I can't afford to travel.
He says to ask for these things.
Ask me to fund the calling on your life
and I will fund all of your flights.
Focus on me. Count on me, and all your wrongs I'll make right.
I'm holding on.
Casting my cares on his shoulders.
He said he can hold them all. So, I've transferred my boulder.
No longer ignoring my gift, but embracing the rise and the falls.
The debt I owe to God is much larger than my credit pitfalls.
How many times must he say serve his people
for me to answer his call?
To trust him to be the lamp to my feet and light to my path?
To believe in his words and fully understand?
That nothing,

not a debt, not a worry, nor a hopeless resolve
is bigger than the one, the creator, the almighty God.
I am His, and as I heed His instructions
I must know,
that every debt will bow low when he tells it to fall.

Busy

Buzzing
Back and forth
Up And Down
Side to Side
Any movement
Anything, but just being
Still
Where I'd have to deal
With all of my feels
Vibrating if I have to
Gently rocking
Anything, but overwhelmed with what's inside
Pinching on my skin
Running
I just wanna hide
Under all the blankets in the dark
Phone off
Not accepting calls
I try it, but you meet me there
Crumbled in a ball
And tell me to come out from there
But I don't trust you
You're just like him
You'll trick me into unraveling

Village Talk

And leave me again
I don't want you near
I'd rather stay in sin
Safe at least
From broken promises
And expectations
Just leave me here
Let me lay
Or let me stay
Busy.

Unbroken

Written for Coco Family Justice Center in support of
survivors of domestic abuse. Though I haven't suffered abuse,
I see blooming yellow roses for the survivors who have.

It's a good thing I don't look like what I've been through
See, someone in my past tried to break my soul
And wither down my beauty like a cast away rose
But my scars are not seen on my face
Exposed for all to see
No, the wounds of my trauma are silenced and tucked deep
Only belted out when I'm prodded or poked to release
My voice to my story
Because there's POWER in shared testimony

See, someone in my past tried to break my soul
But don't pity me
Because I am not broken
I am very much complete
Filled up with inner self love my abuser couldn't beat
And the will to survive that that he couldn't defeat

Through many desolate days I kept believing that I would be free
That my skin would enjoy the light and the warmth on my
cheeks

Village Talk

That laughter would fill my belly when I had nothing to eat
And my faith proved true because I found my release
See
Someone in my past tried to break my soul
But don't pity me
Once bruised, but now healed my strength runneth deep
I learned to fight back and get onto my feet
That strength pushed me to keep fighting and to find
community

What I found in Coco Family Justice Center
can't be contained by a building
It lives in hearts
On faces
In laughter
Through healing
I'm surrounded by people that root for and salute me
People that lead with love
never trying to conform or institute me
Giving me resources to strive and be happy
Ensuring that my victim days are over
and my freedom is long lasting

A community, that has my back as I fight in the courts
Providing free consultations
Advising on restraining orders, but doing nothing by force

Arielle Deseré

A community that links me with others that feel just like me
And gives me tools to cope with my trauma, depression,
and anxiety
Teaching that expression helps to heal and vulnerability isn't
weak
Providing me opportunities
Assuring that my future isn't bleak

See, someone tried to break my soul unsuccessfully
Because this peace that I've pieced together,
people have spent their whole lives
and are out there still seeking
My peace lives in a support system
that's one to be envied

So, though I have a rough past, I don't need to be pitied
I found power by linking arms with the
ones that surround me
And stretching beyond my blood ties to form a new family
These people provide much more than safety
They empowered me to keep fighting

So no, you can't see what I've been through,
and there's a reason
Because inside me is a light so bright
It cannot be extinguished

Village Talk

Yes, someone tried to break my soul, but they failed
and there's a reason

So that someone else suffering could see
that it's not their life story,
but a season

I'm still here
standing victorious
with my foot on the neck of my past
Living out my days full of hope
And no one can ever break that.

Forgiven

Lord knows I don't deserve
Mercy
And yet, I'm still here
But sometimes
I get possessive about forgiveness
As if it's mine to lend.

Living Agape

There're a few people that I need to apologize to
Not because they deserve it
Or I took out on them my attitude
But because I put an expectation on them
that they never signed up to meet
Perfection
And when they didn't meet it
I cursed them and shook the dust off my feet
But I didn't leave it there
I dreamed about it
I screamed about it
I tossed and turned
Got heated
Retreated
And schemed about it
Plotted
How I would make them feel uneasy
I took my heart from them
I completely cut them off
in a way that they could see, but not reach me
living and breathing freely
Striving and constant achieving
Being happy and doing better without them
as if they were beneath me

Arielle Deseré

Life with the windows, closed but the blinds open
The silent treatment
The one that comes with no social media blocks
The one where they can see everything that you're up to
with no restrictions involved
The one where they text and call you,
you read it and decide not to respond
The one that makes you wonder
if the friendship even existed at all
Indifferent
Cold blooded
I even Got indignant
I felt proud of the way I sought revenge
I got haughty with the power
of choosing how relationships end
But as pleasing as it feels to get even
It reveals an ugly truth about me
That I only wanna love
As long as love is loving on me
But Jesus calls for a love that's less of myself
and highly focused on WE
It's not self-centered, easily angered,
it doesn't keep the receipts
Paul said love is patient, love is kind,
it doesn't envy, doesn't boast, it isn't proud,
always protects, always trusts, always hopes

Village Talk

So, if love is an action not a feeling,
that means I have to toughen up
'Cause people won't always treat me good
let alone, go beyond and above
Loving on those who love me?
Even sinners do that
Hugging on those who hug me?
Even sinners do that
Jesus didn't preface his words with this is going to be easy
Or say, only listen if it fits in your personality
'Cause it's easy to love a friend,
but loving someone you hate takes a lotta intentionality
But as his disciple,
the things that I do is how sinners learn about love
And if all the saints love others as ourselves
The world will have more than enough
So, it's up to me to show the world examples of agape love
And if that means I gotta take a couple blows
then I'd better learn to man up
'Cause if I added up all the times I've offended God,
it would overflow the world's supply of measuring cups
So... There're a few people that I need to apologize to
Not because they deserve it
Or I took out on them my attitude
But because I put an expectation on them
that they never signed up to meet

Arielle Deseré

Perfection
And when they didn't meet it
I cursed them and shook the dust off my feet
So, when I'm saying sorry
I'm saying sorry
'cause God doesn't do that to me
No matter what I do,
he still hears and chooses to love up on me
So I'ma follow his example
When he asked Peter do you love me
He told Peter,
"Take care of my sheep."

But Joy

The trees lost a few more leaves today
It rained and it poured
and clouds blocked the sunrays
But joy.
I know about the promises that God makes
So I KNOW as it dries,
I can expect to see
a band of 7 colors in the sky
And every tree will regrow their leaves
and after this season
the flowers will bloom
The wind turns to breeze
It may not be the same as last year
But there will be enough shift
to notice that cold days are over
And summer is here
That's what Joy is.
There's something about being free
When circumstantial happenings don't determine my dreams
It's joy.
Just knowing who's pulling the strings
It's enough to get up and keep moving with ease
Even when
Sometimes, not so easily

I say But joy.
Just knowing that without a doubt
it WILL work out for me
It's not because of the universe or an unnamed HIGHER
being
This peace had a high price and was STILL bought for me
For joy.
With blood, sweat, and tears on a cross
Jesus hung so that EYE
could choose to see
Joy.
Yes, heaven after death
but the knowledge to walk in the now with full victory
That's Joy!
So though I am blemished and unworthy
I am worth SO MUCH more than every part of my story
'Cause joy!
Because now anything I ask in his will, will be given
if I ask of his glory
That's joy.
This smile that I wear daily
The positive outlook that I spread contagiously
This heart to help others along
And to share my hurts with the world unabashedly
Is joy.
It's not being sad

and faking a smile
It's knowing that sad times only last for awhile
It's knowing things will get better in the midst of sorrow
And hoping in today not getting caught up in tomorrow
So, though the trees lost a few more leaves today
And it rained and it poured, and clouds blocked the sunrays
I am reminded of his promises when I see the hard rain,
and I with all of my heart can still say
that God is still good
And choose joy in today
That's joy.

Arielle Deseré

I Didn't Know Him Yet

I've always believed.
Though, I couldn't understand
why when times got tough,
I'd crumble.
Why meditating on scriptures,
tying them into a bundle,
and pinning them to my heart
wasn't enough.
He was real
I knew it.
Because I watched Him save me
I watched him burst into a room
and snatch me from danger
He was real
I knew it.
Because the Holy Spirit would bring chills
And force praise out of my lips
In sad solitude, Jesus would come and sit
Tears would flow, hands would lift
Pure, grateful, unmeasurable worship
Not faked. Unashamed of what others thought
Even in private, he'd give me words to write
Concepts, that I had never been taught
He would show up and he would meet me

Just as far as I sought.
He was surely real
I knew it.
I read all about him and the faith that others lived
But deep, deep, in the crevices of my heart,
I wasn't sure about the Father
That I could trust Him with my weight
That I could trust Him and his way
To jump and not look back
To really not be afraid
That there was no abandonment with Him
And He would never leave.
I read all about the faith that others lived
But my heart just wouldn't let Him be all of that
For Me.

Arielle Deseré

You Touched Me

You set your hand upon my head today.

It felt strange.

Standing there under the weight of your heaviness.

Your might.

Your intentional gravity.

Strength, weighing me down to the depths like an anchor.

Your weight resting on me was an anchor.

And I just felt honored to have you touch me.

With my eyes closed tight and my arms out in reception,

 I wondered if anyone else saw you there.

Pressing on me with your weight as if to say here I am.

Here I am daughter.

I see you.

I've come to let you know that I'm nowhere far.

You are mine.

My hand is on you.

You are chosen.

My very own.

Picked apart.

Your weight so solid I could reach out and hug you.

I wrapped my hand around yours to say I feel you.

To welcome your embrace.

I cried out to worship you, but stopped

and called out to you with simply your name.

And you rejoiced at that.

Tickled that your baby girl could finally understand
that more than I AM,

You're still. And also, and always, my dad.

I can trust you.

I can rest in your arms and fall asleep.

And when I awaken, you'd still be holding me. Never
sneaking off.

Never disappearing.

Always present always still.

Always listening.

Like a wall I can lean on you.

You would never cave like a trick door.

You wouldn't spin around to let me hit the floor.

You are solid.

You are sure.

I can rest all of me on you.

There's nothing you can't take.

Every problem I can bring and like an anchor you remain.

Only love at its purest.

Never malice, never hate.

Even in disappointment you never go, always stay.

So, I wrap my arms around your strength.

And dangle like a kid when they play.

Godzilla.

It's how I feel hanging onto your monstrous glory.

I'm tiny.

So small yet significant clinging onto the mighty.

I can come to you a mess and say dad help me be tidy.

And at my admiration, so childlike,

You are pleased.

I can feel the joy of you delighting.

Proud of your princess.

Your little crafted being.

And I'm here soaking.

Dripping in your peace.

No request needed here.

No asks, I'm complete.

Very plain simply,

I'm just honored that you reached out your hand
and you touched me.

Roar

Lioness of God
Do you know who you are?
Before God formed you in the womb,
He knew you
Before you took a breath, the adversary knew you
Watching like a crow
Waiting for his moment
He watched you stumble
He provided the rocks
He laughed when you fell
Helped when you were mocked
Lioness of God
Do you know who you are?
You think you're a pussy cat
You've lost your roar
You don't know that you hunt
That your paws are made to shred apart
You don't even know you're a lion.
What a shame for the jungle
Waiting for its majesty to remember
Open your mighty jaws
And command for the world to surrender
Roar!

Creator

10 months I formed in my womb
a child in my image.
She is me. Whole being. God like, born able to make another.
A creator, a mother.
I'd walk on unstable ground for her
vision spinning like the world does.
I would push through.
I would grow accustomed.
Just another symptom of creating a woman.
Tailored my body to her needs,
eating all I could see, and tossing up whatever didn't fit.
Boot camp, training for a creature that would push me to my
limits.
She wouldn't come as scheduled.
She would take her time.
She would wait until she was done.
After being pushed she would come. With full force un-assisted.
8 hours un-mediated labor.
I was the doctor and the patient.
Un-medicated.
The pain it took to bear this child.
Walking
Hiking
Pushing through the halls of an apartment.

Village Talk

Grasping walls
Breathing
Pushing
Hiking
Moving through the pain.
Every 2 minutes and lasting for a minute.
Waves of unbearable pain
But I rode the waves for the promise of the love I'd gain.
Rocking in the shower under the crashing water.
Crying out to The Father, "Why have you forsaken me"
Just as his child had done
I felt forsaken
I was shaken, abandoned.
Alone to deal with my pain.
Like Jesus, I recalled that he would come if I called.
He came to me to help me push through.
He held me up to bear it all.
His spirit showed up in
the very same place he told me
I'd be blessed with a miracle
when I was grieving the loss of her brother.
She would be a girl
and I would name her Gabriella.
And now here she was coming full circle.
I was prepared to receive her.
I listened to my instincts.

I knew it was time.

We sped to the hospital to bring forth this miracle of mine.

8 pounds and 6 ounces I pushed out myself.

To see her on my side.

Her eyes staring at mine.

Her arm reaching to touch me.

Every moment I had ever lived was for this baby.

Nothing I had done would ever measure up.

My heart

Had left

My body

And was lying beside me.

Alive alert eyes searching but resting.

I was the Creator

I had made a bless-ing.

A Piece of Me

She loves my stomach as if she misses it there
Like I did my mom
I'd rest my head where
Her navel caved in and her skin rippled naturally
from being stretched to hold, protect, and carry me.
Mama is her safe place
I am her favorite
She hugs me like she wants us to become one again
There's no greater feeling than her love
Running with open arms when I hit the doorway
Being wrapped up in my embrace
Buried in my hugs
This connection, daughter to mother
It's as if she knows she was created from my love
As if she knows she was buried in a womb she can't see.
Like at one, she can remember
that she is a piece of me.

Arielle Deseré

Becoming a Mother

Becoming a mother gave me a new compass
I had to travel life wiser
Left couldn't be a route
The direction became - turn right
Keep my eyes darting
scan the road
Not just ahead
but around and behind
I wasn't just becoming a mother
No
I was raising a woman.

How to Live Dangerously

Creating a little Black woman
So much to teach her in so little time
The world will give her adult treatment long before 25
In our woke and evolved culture,
I fight the urge to tell her don't cry
To be strong
She's okay
To understand what I told her the first time
She is only two, but I expect her to control her anger
She won't be allowed to throw things at daycare with
strangers
Her tears won't win her nice prizes or jobs
Outside,
On a screen
They're looking to rob her innocence
She's only two but she doesn't have long
How do I teach her
To be vulnerably strong
How do I teach her to keep getting up
After being knocked down, cutoff,
emotionally beaten up
I understand why mama said don't cry
Little Black women don't get the luxury of not being tough
But my daughter, our offspring, she is allowed to feel

She is allowed to love her body, have boundaries,
and always keep it real
I tell her she's pretty until she's annoyed
That she's so smart
and can play with the little girls and the boys
While balancing grateful
knowing the women my mother, grand,
and great grands had to be
To navigate a world that wouldn't make space to be free
I'm standing on their shoulders
and lifting up my mini me
She doesn't have to be silenced like in 1963
So, I'm training her to be loud in 2023
A careful balance
I'm choosing to teach her to always live dangerous-ly
So, her daughters can see freedom in 2053
It's my job to push the needle
She should be more courageous than me
She should take more risks
She should exercise free speech
She should not be afraid to create the next big thing
She should break barriers and expect to become CEO
She should grow up creating a corporation of her very own
She's standing on my shoulders and snatching at her dreams
I'm standing on my tippy toes
trying to give her a boost for all the dreams I can't reach

Village Talk

It's NOT her job to see all the things I didn't see
But it's my job to make sure that she has the opportunity
Creating a little Black woman
There's so much responsibility
I have the chance to raise someone that can achieve,
not enough, not almost
but ANYTHING
So, I'm not playing it safe
I'm pushing the boundaries
I'm choosing to teach her
How to live dangerously

Arielle Deseré

Mama is Tired

Beep beep beep
I don't need an alarm
I have a kid
It's the weekend, but there aint no sleeping in
If these kids only knew
What Mama been thru
Maybe they'd get when I peek out of crusty eyes and say,
SNOOZE
Mama is tired
But it don't mean I don't love you
It just means that I'm spent
and out of "how may I help you's"
I don't want to eat at the table and talk about my day
'cause my day is already piled up with complaints
and I don't wanna snap at you right now
so just give me some space
Before I say things I don't mean and you resent me one day
Mama is tired
Let me retreat to my place
Where I can forget that everything really isn't okay
In this bottle
In this weed
In this wooden box TV
Where due dates aint screaming red at me all in my face

Village Talk

The laundry's piling up so now it's laundry day
'cause I decided last weekend that I needed a break
(Heavy sigh)
That's another school night that you'll be out here with me
and up
way way too late
No wonder you're so tired in class
But I'm doing my best to keep you fed and intact
Meanwhile, you sittin' there and got the nerve to look just
like
your dad
As hard as it is
To try to keep a strong face when I'm crumbling within
'cause he told me he'd be here 'til the very end
Now I'm stuck piecing you together from the mess he left us
all in
I wanna run too
I wanna live life for me
When do I get a break from being Mom and Daddy?
Mama is tired
But you don't see and don't know better
So, you hand me homework packets and field trip letters
That come with a fee
That I do not have
And I was trying to make this 20 dollars stretch
for your lunch and my gas

But I have no other choice
I gotta call my dad
And hear disappointment in his tone
As I humble myself to ask for a loan
Mama is tired
And it's not your fault you don't understand
that I can't give you all that I dreamed for
in my backup plan
Mama is tired
But you're hungry so I cannot sleep in
I gotta figure out how to get food back into the fridge
But if you would just understand the hell Mama's been in
You would just let me sleep for 5 more min-utes
Please
Mama is tired

I Am Not Your Superwoman

Damn it!
It was that great great-grandmother of mine
with the 3 kids and breadwinning husband who died
Then left her without a penny to show for her homemaking
That showed my great grand-mother that she would need to do
both the working and baking.
Great-grandmother would push multiple incomes
to build a life for her 5 children, mother, sister, and brother.
Yes, that's what did it.
All that working while keeping the house in order.
All that pushed my grandmother to do the same.
And to do it while she worked
because a man will control you if you let him stake claim.
All that working showed my mother
how to hold it together when her husband was a slave
To vices leaving her with two kids, regret,
a broken heart and some shame.
Yup that's what did it. She never saw a woe is me.
So, she worked, and she cooked running her kids to activities.
Just so I could show my baby girl what it means to cook,
work, never ask, and keep the house clean.
But got dammit, I am not and neither is she!
I will not be your superwoman and nor will she be.
She will be able to cry and ask for help.

She will sometimes drop the ball
and not feel like she's failing herself.
'Cause perfection is a hard act to put on
And it's not fair to ask women to be the backbone
when our backs aren't as strong.
So, I will not be your Superwoman.
I will encourage and nurture.
I will invest my time into making you feel supported.
I will make a home and I will fight for my dreams.
But in this generation, I take my hands off,
and allow you to be king.
I will retire my cape, because I have no desire to be
Superwoman.

Strong Black Man (Mine)

To Mine
The one with broad shoulders
Who carries me on them
Up high
Not allowing me to stumble
Catching me if I slip
Balancing my chaos
Tightening his grip
The definition of
Love is Patient

About Mine
Who loves me through the pain and facades
Strong
Because he never treats our love like a job
But a pleasure
He keeps loving
Through the trauma
Even while feeling misunderstood
Fighting his own demons
If he ever gave up
I know he did the best that he could

But Mine
Still chooses to love

The hell out of me
The imperfect woman
He loves him some me
And I love the hell up out of my king
I was made and he was made
For each other
specially.

Butterflies

I knew he was mine when his lips touched mine and I felt rest
My own, bouncing off of his full lips
and settling like a head on a pillow
He loved me
I suppose because I didn't need him to be complete
See I had been raised in a single parent family
By a mother betrayed not once, but twice
by our two daddies
They promised to love her too
That she was their world
But devastation would soon ensue
Leaving her with two little brown girls
Now it was only her job to teach them the rules
So, she taught us to be strong
To keep going when it seemed hopeless
To be selfless with our future
To make sure our family was well attended
We would eat by any means
We would be humble
We would sleep warm at night,
but know what it was like in the jungle
In the hood everyday
seeing things we wouldn't see where we received mail

We would look at Mama when an outsider asked what we
wanted
And searched her eyes for what her mouth needn't tell
Then always have a backup in case we were disappointed
Like change in our pocket
Some to make a phone call
and some to get us home if we got stranded
She never talked down on any man
But she allowed us to see on our own
And I saw that I could only depend on me
So, when this man kissed me, and I got butterflies
When he kissed me, and I saw stars fall from the sky
When this man kissed me, and my knees buckled
to the sound of my heart on fire
I knew that he was mine
Something I wanted, but didn't need
Like my favorite box of cookies or a B2K CD
I wanted to love him
But I could never give myself fully
Because I could never recall seeing a successful love story
It took time for my shell to soften
And realize I needed him
It was after he helped me see the world in ways I couldn't see it in
His love was way bigger than I had ever dreamed
He knew how to love without requirements
What a powerful thing

Village Talk

A Godly thing
I wanted that
As he peeled back my layers
I started loving back
Being grateful for every little thing
And showing gratitude despite what life may bring
I learned that it takes much more strength
to allow yourself to love
Than to present your heart in a castle
with the guards still up
True love is to be free
Never looking over your shoulder
But around and ahead to the hills
Not worried about what might be coming over
To rest on his lips and feel butterflies
To rest in his presence and feel alive
Is sweeter than any pain on the way
It's worth any risk to feel finally safe
Allowing myself to need him so I can be free
Basking in the Butterflies
Loving fearlessly

"There is no fear in love. But perfect love drives out fear,
because fear has to do with punishment. The one who fears
is not made perfect in love." 1 John 4:18 NIV

This Love

Black.
Blacker than panther black. Blacker than Blue Magic hair grease and hot combs Black. I wear my poof without the slicked down edges. He wears his locs wild like the king of the jungle walking in to work. Black Black.

Love.
Drive through two hours of traffic to sleep with you every day. Come home and cook a meal then love you 'til you don't know what day it is. I just wanna see you happy, love.

Together.
Pick you up outta your downs and drag you until you're uplifted. Rub my feet and when we'd smoke have our blunt ready by the time I'm done cooking. Talk each other into encouragement after another brother is shot down by the police or even by a man than looks like me. We gon' be aight, together.

In Tune.
Good Morning. If ain't nobody got you, I got you. Kiss my tears away. Stay up all night to watch me work. Do you need me to cut the felt? Do you need a glass of water, in tune.

Powerful.

He makes me feel like I can own the world. Like one day the things we dreamed about will come to pass. Like I was meant for you, and you were meant for me, and we were meant to change the world. Like nothing or no one can stop us. Like 10 years isn't enough years. Like let's go buy some property, own some businesses, and rent it out to the block, powerful.

Completed.

Like there is nothing else. There is no one else. This is it for us. There is no soul searching. My soul has been matched and tied to a man whose lips are broad and hands are wide. To a man as black as the night with hair as soft as the clouds in the sky. Whose eyes stare through this hard shell of mine, whose humming voice enlightens my mind. Completed.

This Love.

Blacker than any other. Stronger than Bounty. Deeper than the ocean. Sweeter than blueberries. He is my stronghold. He is my fortress. He is my don't mess up a good thing. I am his Proverbs 31.

This is Black Love.

My momma is gone.

I've just been,
passing time.
Filling up my hole with sand
My life is just a book of empty pages
with you at the beginning and end.

Missing You

I got tired of missing you
I couldn't speak of you without tears
The time kept rolling by
Days kept passing without you here

Missing you didn't bring you back
So, I started speaking you up
I brought you into the spaces you would've been
I passed around your name like hugs
But it wasn't enough...

So, I made people remember your smile
We laughed about your temper and how you could go bad easily
We talked about the look you'd give
We traded memories

But I wanted to see you
So, I hung up all your pictures
I wrapped my head in your scarves
I wore your things I had but never mentioned
And I looked in the mirror...

But it didn't lend me your ears
So, I made you come alive

Arielle Deseré

I let go of the things I was sorry for
Then allowed myself to feel your presence
So, I could apologize

But it didn't resurrect your wisdom
So, I accepted you're always with me
I hear your teachings when I need correcting
When I cry, I feel you kiss me

But I resented my lack of honor to you
Because your spirit is way too strong
Too special to pretend it doesn't exist
Suppressing our memories began to feel wrong

The days without you here are long
The pain just doesn't fade
I wish that you were here
But your memory I refuse to erase

I've grown tired of missing you
I wanna live with you and all of your greatness
It's too cold here without your warmth
Your life is worth embracing

So, I'm bringing you back to me
I'm speaking out your name

Village Talk

I'm sharing your life with others
I'm loving through the pain

But it's not enough to keep me happy
So, I'm bundling up my depression
 I'm turning my sorrow into motivation
Because waiting around to see you takes so much patience

I still smell you when I bury my face in your beanies
Even if the scent is long gone, the sensation stays with me

Your smile is still infectious
I beam whenever I see it
New long-lost pictures make me feel like
a piece of you is still living

Accepting that you're gone doesn't make you go away
But not talking about you, does makes your memory fade
So, I'm talking about you now, as much as it hurts
Monica, Mommy, Sister, Daughter, Auntie
I promise to never let you go
I love you Mama.

Family is Everything

One thing about it
Whether it's only for funerals
Birthdays
and Holidays
Or an everyday reality
Your family will always be your family
Despite offense
It's a constant that won't change
The memories
The good times
and the warmth that comes with
Will get you through the rain.

Note of Love: If you don't have a family, or have been harmed to the point of danger, Christ died and gave you new brothers and sisters. It's so much easier to be tormented in isolation. Get in community.

Homemade Holiday

Aint no "chestnuts roasting on an open fire"
But the house smells like ham hocks and sweet potato pie
Last night, I ate to get full because the kitchen would be closed
from as early as 5
And if I'm up early, and I'm lucky,
I'll get to test if the dishes taste right
Bragging rights
to assure the fam they're in for a good dinner tonight
We might be hungry
But the anticipation
makes it all worth the wait
Like a fast,
I'm replacing hunger with cousin time
and a smile on my face
My nephew running around playing his Nintendo
like I was back in the day
And my brother passing around spirits
to everybody of age
Here comes Unc with a bottle of something
that only gets cracked on holidays
And my messy auntie that comes empty handed,
but always got something to say
We passing time making the kids show us that dance
they be doing these days

101

And all the men gathered around the TV
arguing about some football game
Joy is in the air
'cause all the family is in the same place
Catching up on everything
we missed since the last holiday
Dinner time has passed
But we still waiting.
We've learned patience
'cause we know that the wait
will be well worth the waiting
The funny auntie just arrived
always late, but on time for instigating
Luckily,
we already separated my uncles
from their loud and heated debating
Finally! The cousins come with the rolls
back from their trip to the store
Smelling like 5 different perfumes
and laying low 'cause they've done this before
The matriarch gives them the look
snatches the rolls
And announces wash up
'cause it's time to eat
And we gather holding hands
while our noses smell three different meats

Village Talk

Cousin Reverend So and So prays hard
and long enough to cover us in-to the next year
And it's a good prayer,
but we all show we're thankful it's over by saying
"AMEN" with great cheer
And for the first ten minutes, we experience
a total shift in the room's atmosphere
Silence,
forks clinking
"Mm mms" here and there
No complaints. Just satisfaction.
The food was just as we thought
To go plates with foil lids
hid in the oven, in the fridge, and on the top
A million kisses and drawn-out goodbyes
remarking on how nobody fought
What a time!
The cameras followed all the commotion,
and a few moments were caught
But like the time put into the meal,
it was about the family memories.
You had to be there.
Some moments can't be re-lived, or store bought.

Aviana's Song – King's Daughter

She looks forward
Assured
Un-intimidated by impossible
She moves with resilience
Well ahead of tomorrow
Past the popular
Knowing
To take her place at the front
Settling into the place that most others want
The throne
Opposite the crowd
Living abundant
Joyous out loud
Her name means freedom
To breathe
Be alive
And she glows brightly
While the curious are drawn to her light
She listens to God's whispers
And jumps
Into the unknown
As onlookers watch
And stalk from their phones
Waiting to see if she lands safely

Village Talk

Peeking
peeping
watching her glide
whispering
Reluctant to jump themselves, but not blind
They gawk in awe
sometimes envy
as she lands every time
It's not luck
She says,
It's her faith
Proven true every time
And for obedience, rewards
Walking what true faith looks like
It's her purpose
She's ministering by walking in faith
And the people learn from the moves that she makes
Despite risks, she expects to see grace
Because she knows who she is and is assured of her place
She's fully aware of her place in line
And of her inheritance
As a King of Kings' child
Each time higher
Farther
A bit more steep
But living out louder

Happier
A bit more free
Living exactly who God named her to be
Aviana
To live
To radiate
To breathe.

Mirror Mirror

Mirror Mirror
What do you see?
Little Black child. You ask what I see when you walk past me?
I see a brown skinded, light skinded, dark skinded queen
I know society says otherwise,
but the truth is
people yearn for your beauty
They spend thousands for your features,
but don't want your life journey
See
But something about your melanin, it tells a story
Bruised, but not broken
Pushed, but not folded
Creased, but not crumpled
Deeply complicated, but beautiful to all that behold it
You work harder than your peers
and are robbed of opportunities
when you know you deserved it
Your story is one of resilience
Your trials fuel your trendsetting creativity
which reveal the depths of your brilliance
You. are. magnificent!
Effortlessly...
That voice in the back of your head that says you

will never make history
is a liar
You will shine, you will fly, you will set this world on fire.
You are a doctor, you are a singer
You must speak what you aspire
As a child of the most high,
you have full access to ask and receive
all that you desire
So, ask for the world
Achieve and inspire
Reach for the stars
Build your empire
You will succeed
No matter what people say
You will be
No matter how long it takes
You can reach all of your dreams
No matter how far away
Your future can be made
If you work hard and you pray
So, it doesn't matter
if you were born in the 'burbs or made in the streets
You hold your head high
and practice that speech
'Cause nothing can keep you
from your victory

Village Talk

So, the next time you walk past THIS mirror
You STOP
What do you see?
Mirror mirror
You're looking at
A champion
An achiever
A winner
A king.

Roar Pt. 2

Arielle
Lioness of God
Now do you know who you are?
When you stand in the mirror
And you claim to love the woman that you are
Do you see past hurt
and the pain and the scars?
Will you keep them to yourself
or will you open up your jaws?
Don't be a pussycat
Don't keep freedom to yourself
Make certain that when you walk into a room,
you share the abundance of your words
It's where the Lord placed your wealth
You had better,
And I mean you had better
Roar!

Predestined Victory

I woke up this morning
and with the breath in my lungs,
I spoke to the creation I made:
Wake up child. Go forth victorious in your day.

For I once spoke that I would be a mother
and God made a way
I spoke that I would share my gift
with the whole wide world
and He gave me an Instagram page

Formed from dust,
but inspired by his very face
He gave me the power to speak life
and seek wisdom for every decision I make
Then showed me that there are no limits
and the boundaries I imagined
can be praised and shouted away

That means I have the keys to every door
every gate
every barrier blocking my way

Just as fulfilling as my words are

to bring forth inspiring dreams,
My words can sabotage
holding me back from bless-ed things

That negative talk wrapped in fear
is only as powerful as my lips and thoughts allow
So, I'm mindful of what I consume
because what goes in must come out

Those that are called, have been crowned
We already wield the power offered to us
by the luring snake on the ground
It's already ours
There's no offer to make
If we replace self-fulfillment with love,
the blessings are already coming our way

Speak the words of victory to that thought
that says you don't have the energy,
the brains,
the funds to succeed
And the enemy of deceptive thoughts
has no choice but to flee
For you are worthy of marvelous things
And joy cannot be stolen,
as long as you believe

No matter how bad it looks right now,
the good prevails in the end
Armed with that knowledge,
what's keeping you from going for your win?

Take it.
For it was written for you to succeed
long before you even begin.

Genesis 1:27, Proverbs 2:6, Proverbs 14:6, Proverbs 15:14,
Proverbs 19:2, Hebrews 11:30, Isaiah 54:17, James 3:3-12,
Genesis 1:28, James 1:5, Romans 8:28, Matthew 6:33,
Matthew 4:3-11, Romans 8:39

Heir (Purpose)

Hello Queen
I hear your salute
The respect is pleasing so I return the same to you
Hello King

But I wonder,
If the title is to say "Hey Black Girl"
 or a reminder of the truth
Are you looking at me
speaking over my past?
As if you see beyond the imperfections
and the scabs

Do you see royalty
and attach my worth to a tag?
Or are you simply using "Queen"
because you don't know who I am
You see the light,
but struggle to identify
what you feel but can't explain
'cause you don't see it with your eyes

An heiress
made by a power transcending logic,
space and time
My inheritance is creation

The ground, the beasts, the things that fly

Everything my father made,
the earth and fullness there inside

It's everlasting
It reaches to the heavens
And I can pull his goodness in
whenever I seek out his blessings
'Cause he loved, he sent his son
to restore the line of succession
Then left me with his spirit
to hear HIS plans of manifesting

That's called His Will.
Along with his spirit,
he put power in my hands
And armed me with his word
and plus a matching gift of Gab
A sword that strikes like lightening
To knock down Giants where they stand
And a faith that makes earthquake
with just the mention of my Dad

You see the throne in me,
and say "Queen"
'Cause you can't name it,
can't explain
But that's the spirit telling you,

that I'm your sibling,

we're the same
This gift you see me using,
you have too
It just looks different
It's in the place you left it on the shelf,
the gift kept hidden

The seed that grows so easy,
bearing fruit although refused
The one people have told you
that they see inside of you
The one you may not love and so
you're too stubborn to use
So instead, you roam earth blindly
wondering what you're here to do.

Listen to me King
I'm speaking to you truth
You're dying to know why you're alive,
but there's HEIR inside of you
Remember whose you are
and walk upright in majesty
It's connected to your purpose
you keep claiming you don't see
Revisit what God gave you
and go multiply that thing

And as you exercise your gifts

Have faith that you'll begin to see
Watch how as you pray,
Earth will align with all your dreams
The thing you thought you didn't love,
will evolve into vision
Because creation will flow from you
into the world with just a mention

Stop wandering Queen
You're called,
bear fruit
step out the wilderness
The moment you found Jesus,
you inherited dominion
Everything you see is yours,
rule the earth as God intended

And as you call out "King" and "Queen,"
don't lose sight of the connection
to ascension
There's power in those words
I hear co-heir when "Queen" is mentioned.

"For you did not receive the spirit of slavery to fall back into fear, but you have received the Spirit of adoption as sons, by whom we cry, "Abba! Father!" The Spirit himself bears witness with our spirit that we are children of God, and if children, then heirs – heirs of God and fellow heirs with Christ, provided we suffer with Him in order that we may also be glorified with Him."

Romans 8:15-16 ESV

Letter to The Village

Thank you for flipping through these pages. I pray that as you read, you felt my heartbeat. If even just one of these poems made you feel seen, I ask that you share this book with someone else. Get it into their hands and give them a warm welcome into The Village.

About the Author

Arielle Deseré is a poet and spoken word artist born and raised in the San Francisco Bay Area. She holds a Bachelors degree from the HBCU, Norfolk State University and Master of Art in TV and Film from San Diego State University. She is a wife, mother, community activist, and lover of Christ Jesus. All of which greatly influence her writing.

Arielle has been writing and reciting poetry since the age of 12. In middle school, she began performing in front of crowds, being called upon to perform for events at both school and church. In adulthood, she has been commissioned to write and perform at various events: such as the 2021 ACLU Nor Cal Conference, Women in Artificial Intelligence Ethics Tech & Tools Conference, Contra Costa Board of Supervisors Meetings, and the Black Minds Matter 2 Training for the American Psychiatric Association.

Arielle is using her poetry for her own inner healing and moving others to seek healing for themselves. Her writings focus on the lived Black experience, often allowing her passion for social justice to ring out and evoke emotion. According to Arielle, the role of art in social action is to report and reflect. She believes she is doing that by moving people to open their minds, react, and take-action for change.

Special Thank You & Recognition

To My Cover Artist – Thank you so much for your beautiful and diligent work. You patiently heard my vision and made it happen. She can be found on Fiverr: Sanagraphics09

Nazma – Thank you for helping me through this process, formatting my book, and bringing my poetry to life on the pages. She can be found on Fiverr: @nazma_formatter

Dominque Calder – Thank you for being the first to flip through these pages and brainstorm cover ideas.

Auntie Gigi Crowder - Thank you for believing in me and calling on me to share so much of my work.

Grace Bible Fellowship of Antioch (Pastor Smith & Lady Q) – Thank you for seeing the gift in me as a child and giving me a platform.

Monique "Moe Ministry" McCoy – I truly appreciate your encouragement as I embarked on this book journey. Your generous advice and wise words gave me direction.

Arielle Deseré

Made in the USA
Columbia, SC
18 November 2024

46834496R00079